THE SONG OF THE CAPTIVES

A VERSE ADAPTATION OF TESTIMONY TAKEN FROM DETAINEES AT ABU GHRAIB PRISON

JABEZ L. VAN CLEEF

For Prisoners of Conscience.

Books by Jabez L. Van Cleef

On Human Rights and Civil Disobedience

The Palimpsest of Human Rights
The Song of the Captives
All One Family Sing
The Birth of Propaganda

More Books by Jabez L. Van Cleef

On Mysticism in the Anglican Tradition

The Song of the Cloud of Unknowing
The Song of Angels
The Showing of Love
The Fire of Love

Verse Adaptations of Judeo-Christian Texts

Gospels in Verse
The Saxon Gospel
The Song of the Thunder
The Song of Thomas
The Book of Ashes
The Song of Judith
Three Liturgical Plays

Secular Poetry and Fiction

Painkillers
Heaven On Earth
It Rhymes With Breath: Five Stories of Death
Trust Me On This One: Three Stories of Betrayal
Children of Wrath
Left Eye/Right Eye & In the Belly

On Indigenous Cultures and World Religions

All Is Beautiful: The Navajo Creation Story
God Wears Many Skins
He Kumulipo
The Tawasin of Mansur al-Hallaj
The Alchemy of Happiness
The Unstruck Drum of Eternity: Poetry of Kabir
The Song of Confucius
Igbo Singing, and Three Igbo Stories
Nanai and The Quest for the Fire Bird

Published by Spirit Song Text Publications
20 Pine Avenue, Madison, New Jersey 07940

Library of Congress Cataloging-in-Publication Data
The Unstruck Drum. English
The Song of the Captives: Poetic Paraphrase of Testimony by Prisoners at
Abu Ghraib
by Jabez L. Van Cleef
ISBN 1438221088 (paper).
EAN-13 9781438221083.
I. Van Cleef, Jabez L. 1948-   . II. Title
2 4 6 8 9 7 5 3
Printed in the United States of America

Contents

Note: The poetry in *The Song of the Captives* is based on sworn statements obtained at Baghdad Correctional Facility, Abu Ghraib, Iraq, January 16-21, 2004, and obtained by the Washington Post. The full text of these depositions appears in *Torture and Truth*, by Mark Danner, pp. 225-248.

AMEEN

Here I am among prisoners,

Arrested by the foreign soldiers.

They brought me out here in restraints.

At first they put me in their tents.

The first night was the longest night,

Because the guards interrupted it:

They came in, every hour or two,

With threats of things that they would do:

Torture, and other punishment;

For all these men were violent.

The second day, before it was night,

They transferred me to the hard site.

Before I went into this place

They put a sand bag over my face,

Over my head; I could not see

Anything that would happen to me.

First they took all of us inside

And started to scream very loud.

They stripped my skin naked and raw,

And asked me if I pray to Allah.

I told them, Yes, I pray to him.

They said, Fuck you, and then fuck him.

They said, You are not leaving here

Healthy, we'll take that little pecker,

We're looking for something to chop,

We'll give you a little handicap.

One of them said, You have a wife?

I said, Yes, and I fear for her life.

He said, If your wife ever saw it,

Like this, with you all smeared in shit,

She would not think you're such a man.

Another said, If I saw your wife,

She would not fear to lose her life,

She would not have a thing to fear,

She'd only know joy and pleasure,

Because I would be raping her.

One of them took me to the shower;

Where we were alone, together;

When he took the bag from my head

I saw him looking at me, naked.

He was big and strong, a black man:

He told me to get nice and clean,

He would rape me for his own pleasure,

And I was very scared in there.

But it was only a kind of threat;

When I came out of there, still wet,

They put the sand bag back on me,

And as we walked I heard them say

They would take me to cell number five,

This is where I was going to live.

For five days there I did not sleep

Because the men would wake me up;

They came at will there, in and out,

And would not let me lie or sit:

They forced me to stand still in place

For hours under the threat of force.

They slammed the metal outer door,

Every time they would slam it louder.

The black man took me to the shower;

I washed, and he would stand and stare.

They started to interrogate me.

Sometimes at first I told a lie—

When I said I had lied to them,

They said worse punishment would come.

Then other questioners came in:

At first, seeming reasonable men,

They said, If you tell us the truth,

We will let you practice your faith,

We will free you soon as we can,

You will leave here before Ramadan.

So I confessed, told all of it.

New people came four days after that;

I went to another camp somewhere;

I didn't see these men any more.

New people came with more questions.

Rules, threats, and interrogations.

After everything I had said,

Now they accused me of having lied.

After eighteen more days of this,

They sent me back to where I was.

I asked them why I was going back,

They said, Who knows, and, What the fuck.

Two days before Ramadan was over,

There was another interrogator
Who came to me with a woman
And told me I better come clean,
That I was only one step away
From being in prison until I would die.
This he said twice, at the beginning,
And at the end of his questioning.
When the end of Ramadan came,
Instead of leaving and going home,
I did leave, I got shot to hell,
And I was transferred to the hospital.

In the ward I saw one of them
Called Steve, a soldier who came
Threatening me, when I would go back,
That he would find which bones to break,
And apply hard torture on me,
And I would never get away.
I said, I am sorry what happened.
He said, Don't you be sorry now,
You will be sorry when I own you.
He said, If I give you some torture,

What do you think? Would that be fair?

I asked him, Why torture me then?

He said, We need more information.

I had already told them all I knew.

He said, We'll see, when we get you.

So then, less than three weeks later

I went back to the interrogator,

To Abu Ghraib, and when I got there,

The guard put a pistol by my ear,

He said, I will kill you right now,

Not one person will ever know.

At Abu Ghraib I spent the night

Then went next day to the hard site.

The soldiers there came all around

They screamed and shoved me to the ground.

The broken bone in my leg hurt,

I had to walk from the far gate,

If I didn't walk, they would beat it.

I was in bad shape in my cell.

They took my crutches, made me crawl.

The soldiers took all that I had;

They took my clothes, left me naked.

I had no blanket, nothing left,

Every hour they came in to see,

Threatening to kill me, torture me,

Send me to Guantanamo Bay,

So I would never get away.

One man said, I tried to shoot you,

I missed you, but I'll get you now,

That gimpy little leg in a cast,

I don't think you can run so fast.

We'll toss a knife into your cell

Then shoot your ass as quick as hell.

We'll let you live, on second thought,

You're such a worthless piece of shit.

We'll make you wish that you had died,

But it won't happen.

So he said.

The night guard came in with his friends:
They held my mouth wide with their hands
And placed pork and liquor inside it;
This made my stomach want to vomit.

On my forehead and on my nose
They smeared a hot thick kind of grease,
Some of them held me down on my back,
Others hit me with a plastic stick,
There on my leg, where the wound was,
And one told me his reason for this:
He had been wounded in his leg too;
He needed revenge, and I would do.
They stripped me naked on the bedcover
And said they'd rape me all together:
One of the men took a marker,
And drew a woman picture, a whore,
Just over the crack on my lower back,
And he poked at it with his plastic stick,
He said it was not big enough,
He wanted a wider hole to stuff;
Next to the bed, he made me bend,
Holding my buttocks one in each hand.
When he had me where he wanted,
Then, he asked me if I repented.
He said, Do you believe anything?
I believe in Allah, I told him.

He said, Well, I believe in torture;
Let's see if torture or Allah is stronger.

They put my hands in cuffs, behind,
Locked me to the bed, at one end,
So I would hang there from my arms;
Then they ordered me, Curse Islam;
They hit me where my leg was broken,
So I obeyed and cursed my religion;
They said, Thank Jesus, we didn't kill you!
I did all they told me to do.
This was against my deep belief,
But my arms were painful and stiff.
They let me hang there from the bed,
And I lost knowledge what I did;
Lost consciousness, and slept there, hanging,
And woke again, my body dangling.

There was numbness on my right side,
No feeling there, three fingers dead;
I pulled myself up, on the bed:
One of the soldiers came and peed.

He yelled, squirting his urine on me,

Towelhead peed on himself, come see!

They came and had their laugh, and left,

In a few hours, took the cuffs off.

But every day it would start over,

With a new interrogator,

Coming in to humiliate me,

Threatening me more, every day.

They hung me up from the cell door:

I couldn't take it any more.

I told them about the doctor,

Who said I had a broken shoulder,

If you lift up my arms behind,

He said the bone would break again,

He told me that the bones would break,

Don't put my arms behind my back!

But then they hung me from the door

All night long, hour after hour,

I was hanging up there again,

Screaming and hoarse from all that pain,

And the guard said, I don't care,

There's no one but these shits to hear.

In the morning he comes again,

Asking, like a joke, Are you in pain?

Yes, I said, Yes, I am, yes, yes;

That's what we want, that's good, he says.

Then he smacked my head some more,

Left me hanging there on the door.

Then the next day the doctor came,

I told him that my hand was numb,

I thought my shoulder was broken;

He said, I'll get another opinion,

He brought another doctor in

Who said an Xray should be taken.

And when it was, they told me again,

Your shoulder is not really broken,

But there is a ligament torn.

They took me back to the hard site,

And dropped me off there by the gate.

I have to crawl back to my cell

Because I can't walk even a little.

The soldiers took away my clothes

And left me there naked like this.

Then other soldiers come here at night,

I wake up to a flashing light:
They are taking photos of me
While I am lying naked this way.
They think I know some guy with guns,
And keep on with interrogations,
Isn't he in these pictures here?
What is his name, do you remember?
They say they'll come here every night
Until I get this answer right;
They point their weapons at my head
And threaten they will kill me dead.
They hang me up there on the door
So my feet barely touch the floor;
Sometimes they bring their snarling dogs,
They snap and bite at my bare legs.
I hang there with my arms behind,
Drive the snarling out of my mind,
For I have told them all I know,
And I don't know what else to do.

ABDOU

On the third day, in the afternoon,
There was an interrogation.
The soldier came into my cell,
And led me away down the hall,
To room number thirty-seven,
The shower room for detainee men,
And he started to punish me.
There was hitting with a baton,
And with the hands of several men,
And then they brought a box of food
Placing it next to where I stood.
Then they made me climb up on it
And stand naked, except a blanket.
Then a tall black soldier came
Bringing tools and wires with him:
He attached electrical wires
To some of my toes and fingers;
I could feel part of what he did;
There was a bag over my head,

I could not see where the man was.

He put another wire on my penis.

And I heard them talk for a while,

And I waited standing very still,

Wondering what would happen to me;

And then I heard one of them say,

Where's the power switch anyway,

Does this room have electricity?

And I waited more, wondering,

In fear, with all my sweat trickling...

Suddenly he took this bullhorn thing,

And shouted until my ears rang;

And then they brought a camera

And they took some pictures of me;

I knew because I saw the light,

The flash, and I was waiting for it,

The shock, when they turned on the power,

And I stood there waiting for an hour.

One of them took the hood off me,

He told me, Stand here, in this way,

Stand and do what I tell you to do,

And I will take a portrait of you.
I held this pose for a long time,
But then fell down in front of him,
I was very tired, I fell down;
I lay on the floor before these men;
They made me stand carrying a box
On the stairs till I strained my back;
I dropped the box out of my hand,
Then they screamed at me again,
But still I couldn't understand,
I didn't understand a word,
So then they put back on the hood.
Then they made me lift a white chair
High over my head and hold it there.
But I was getting tired again,
So then again the chair came down.
They took the hood off, one of them,
And they took me back to my room.
I slept there for about an hour,
I woke up very soon after,
It was headcount time, I got up,
Then I couldn't go back to sleep,

I was very scared lying there,

Thinking about my penis and that wire.

THAAR

I went to the solitary

September tenth, two thousand three.

I was there sixty-seven days.

I only saw my own suffering

And I do not know anything

Of the torture that others got.

There was very little to eat,

And the main guard who came to me

Cuffed my hands to the door each day.

But when his duty had ended,

There came to me a different guard.

He released the cuff from my hand,

Then he twisted my arms around,

And cuffed them together behind.

I asked him please to release me,

I should not be punished this way,

I did not do anything bad,

But on my chest, he hit me, hard,

Cuffed me to the window to hang,

About five hours, all for nothing,
And I did not get food that day;
There was no food till the next day.

In the first days of Ramadan
I saw them take many people down;
In the gallery, between the cells,
We could see them and hear their calls.
Lots of people getting naked,
Being punished for what they did.
They piled their bodies in pyramids,
And made them stand up wearing hoods.
There were two boys in that place,
Cuffed together and face to face,
Naked, and a soldier beat them,
And a big crowd was watching him,
And they took pictures of these two,
The top and bottom of their torso.
And there were three female soldiers
Laughing at these boy prisoners.
These two boys were young, both of them,
But I did not know them by name.

ABD

One day when they searched in my cell,

They found a broken toothbrush handle.

They made a note how sharp it was,

And said I would attack the police;

They punished me and locked me down.

I swear that toothbrush was not mine.

They said to me, We will take away

Your clothes and mattress for six days,

We will not punish or beat you.

But the next day the guard came through

And he cuffed me to my cell door

And left me cuffed there for two hours;

They took me into a closed room:

While I was there five guards came.

First they poured cold water on me,

Then they made me squat down this way

By a pail filled with some urine,

And I had to put my head in,

Then with a broomstick they beat me,

And one put his foot up this way,

On my neck, to push my head in,

Holding it down under the urine.

Then I lay down on my face naked,

And they spit around my buttocks,

And then they spit on the broomstick,

They rubbed it around my anus,

I could feel them ready to press,

But it was only a kind of threat,

They did not really insert it.

And a female soldier was there,

I had never seen her before;

She stood on my legs to hold them,

But they lost interest in the broom.

They took out some big loudspeakers,

And shouted at me for three hours,

And it was very cold in there,

And I was shivering, I remember.

They gave me clothes during the day,

And at night they took them away,

And the truth is, after three days,

They gave me back my clothes and mattress,

They didn't finish the whole six days,

And I am very grateful for this.

ASAD

November fifth, two thousand three,

The U. S. forces transferred me,

To Isolation, over here.

When they took me out of the car,

A prison soldier hit me here,

Struck me with his hand on my face,

And they took off all my clothes.

They made me crawl down the hallway,

And I had to keep on this way.

There were many cuts in my skin,

On my knees and my chest and hands,

I was bleeding, the floor was wet

With the blood from where I was cut.

They stopped and locked me up again,

But an hour later they came in,

They took me to the shower room,

So I washed in the cold water,

And came out to the hall after.

They made me stand on a box naked,

And they hit me on my manhood.

I don't know what they hit me with,

I fell down on the floor beneath,

I could not lie there on the floor,

They made me crawl around some more.

Then they tied up my hands behind,

In the morning they released my hands,

And took me into my cell here,

And gave me back my clothes to wear.

Two days later they all came in,

And gave me my interrogation.

The soldier in charge grabbed my head,

Pushed it into the wall by the bed,

Then he tied my hands to the bed,

And left me there without any food.

Two days later the men came in,

Took my mattress away again,

And took my clothes away with it.

I had to sleep on a jump suit,

For three days more until they came

And gave these back a second time.

SHALAN

There came a day when guards began
To torture us, every one:
In this they followed three men,
And this is how their work was done:
They took first Amjid Iraqi,
And they took all his clothes away.
Then they beat him till he passed out,
And I saw the result of it,
When they took the hood from his head,
His face and head were all in blood.
Then they took his body away
To solitary confinement bay,
And those living there would report
That the guards beat him every night.

The evening shift was very sad,
As we suffered with the night guard.
They brought in three captives handcuffed
To each other, and then they pushed
One on top of the others to look

Like they are gay and having sex;
When they refused, the guard beat them
Until they got back one on the other,
And then they took a flash picture.
After that they beat up Asad,
They had a food box where he stood.
First they poured water on him,
Although it was the coldest time,
They would beat him on his shrunk dick
And give his testicles a kick,
They put rubber gloves on their fists,
And punched him in the private parts,
And handcuffed him to the cell door
And left him without food and water.

After that time they brought young boys
And poured water from the galleries,
From the second floor, cold water,
Until one started to cry out,
He was screaming, saying, My heart!
They brought the doctors to treat him,
And thought he was dying on them.

After this they brought six people,
And beat them up until they fell,
And one of them, his nose was cut,
And lots of blood was running out,
He screamed but they didn't hear it,
These three men who were doing it.
The doctor came to stitch the cut.
The main guard asked how to do that,
And it's true, the doctor showed him
How to make stitches on the man,
The soldier took needle and string,
And himself finished the stitching.
And another soldier came there,
And he took a picture of it:
The prisoner there with his new cut,
Stitched by the same one who gave it.

Then they beat up all of the others
Until they were lying on the floor;
Every time one would fall down
A guard would pull him up again,
Drag them up to stand on their feet

Swaying and tilting left and right;
The head guard beat the Syrian
With so much enthusiasm
We thought he might have lost his mind,
And that this beating would not end;
The Syrian, all naked, ran upstairs,
And down the hall so that the others
In all their cells could see him run,
Then they shut him away again.
Four days they poured water on him,
He couldn't sleep through that whole time;
They hanged him from the foot of the bed,
And he screamed but no one answered.

A translator was helping them,
Abu Adell the Egyptian:
Like they watched live movies
Of this man arranging the bodies:
The three young guys being piled up
So one was balanced on the top,
All arranged by this translator
So that they could take a picture.

I tell you this is what I saw

And I remember this to be true.

NORI

In Ramadan, I forget the date,
We were involved in a dispute,
So they moved us to the hard site.

As soon as we captives arrived,
They put sandbags over our heads,
Then they beat us with plastic sticks,
And made reference to our sex,
Calling us all abusive things
And other humiliating.
They took the sandbag off my head,
And made me get completely naked.
They ordered me to hold my penis
And stroke it to and fro like this,
Came with a camera in the night,
To take our pictures doing it,
As if it was some kind of porn
And we were animals, not human.

No one showed us mercy then,
There were only beatings and pain,

And cursing; they would write foul things
On our buttocks with their black pens,
Which we didn't know what it means.
They left us all for two whole days
Naked, no clothes, no mattresses,
As if we were dogs or even worse,
And every night a soldier guy
Came and beat us mercilessly,
We were all handcuffed to the bed
Till he left at oh four hundred.
He did this for three days or more
And he never gave us our dinner.
All we ever got was bread and tea,
The chicken and things, he threw away.

The first night when they stripped us naked
They made us get in a pyramid,
We were down on our hands and knees,
Piled one on the other like this,
And they took pictures front and back,
Showing our sex and the ass-crack,
And if you want to see details,

Ask the night guard to show you this.
During the day they gave us clothes,
But when the night guard came to us,
He took the clothes, left us naked,
And he handcuffed us to the bed.
In the morning he uncuffed us,
Hit us in the head and the face,
Punched us in the stomach some more,
Then he goes home and leaves us there.

I kept thinking during the day
What is in the mind of this guy?
What is he going to do to us,
The white man with the white glasses?
When I see him, I'm scared to death,
I can hardly take my own breath.
Watch the pictures among his things.
He came with two female soldiers,
And with a black soldier, together,
And it was during the long, dark night,
We did filthy things I regret,
We were naked, he made us stroke it,

Holding the penis, then we jerk it,

Then he would bring another captive,

His mouth all coated with saliva,

On his knees down in front of me,

And on one side a soldier would be

There with a camera, taking pictures,

To look like his mouth was on my penis.

After this they brought my friend, Hashim,

And tried to force me to slap him.

I told them, No, he is my friend;

So they forced him to hit me instead,

But Hashim and I agreed before

He punches my stomach, and no more,

For neither wanted punishment for

Refusing to punish the other.

Yet I was beaten when I said, No,

And beaten again for sparing Mustafa,

Hussein, Nori, Saleh, Hiadar,

Hathem, Ahmed, and several more,

These are the names of who was there,

During this long night of our torture,

Which was only one long night,
But felt like a thousand years of shit.

I do not know the name of the soldier,
The one who was night supervisor,
But I know him to look at him:
He is a white, muscular man,
Wearing clear medical glasses,
A blue tattoo on one of his shoulders,
He comes every night, others with him,
They stay from 4 p. m. to 4 a. m.

MUSTAFA

Just two days before Ramadan
A group of soldier guards came in,
Bringing in for us two prisoners
As example for our behavior.
They made these two become all naked;
When they were this way beat their heads,
And one of them bled quite freely
From a cut he got over his eye.
They called in the doctor to stitch it,
And he sewed it while they all watched,
Then after the doctor was done,
They started beating him again.

They removed all my clothes also,
For seven days I was naked too,
And they brought a group of people
To observe me in my cell.
One prisoner was a civil case:
Three guards presented him to us.
They beat him and took off his clothes,

And stuck a wire into his ass,

Then they took some pictures of this.

The head guard cuffed the prisoners

And hung them from the doors and windows

In a manner that tore their muscles;

For several hours we heard their voices

Screaming and wailing in the hallways.

One day they brought six generals

From the former leader's army:

These they made naked just as well,

Took pictures, and tortured them all,

And they enjoyed themselves with this,

As if entertaining visitors.

When the army doctor came in

To stitch the injured captive men,

The head guard became excited

And he took the needle and thread

To stitch the cut he had just made.

They would beat some very hard,

Using a stick, and if they injured,

They would call the same doctor in,

But then beat the same man again.
Some they pissed on after they beat,
And we heard them screaming all night.

Here I would like to make a point
Which to my mind is important:
There were three guards who did these things.
The other guards were very good
And with them I could hold up my head.
The captives like them and respect them,
And were happy when they would come.
The others give a good image
And do not treat us like garbage;
They show there is a big difference
Between your country and our former rulers.

Again, the time before Ramadan,
These three guards shut the prisoners in,
They covered the doors of the men
With bed sheets, so they couldn't be seen.
I heard some screams from down below
Room number one, I was in fifty,

Right above it, so I could see.

Through a grate, I saw the head guard,

In the room below, the man was naked,

The guard had a phosphoric light,

Next to the man's ass he held it,

And he stuck it into his ass,

So the man screamed for help to us;

There was another guard helping him,

And a female soldier had come,

Taking pictures of this activity;

The man is still there, you can verify.

HUSSEIN

I was in the solitary.

Me and my friends were treated badly.

The soldiers took all of our clothes

Even our underwear, off us,

And they beat us up very hard,

And they put hoods over our head.

When I said to them, I am sick,

They laughed and hit me with a stick.

They beat me, and they brought my friend,

And told him, Here is where you stand,

And brought me, saying, Here, kneel down,

In front of him, with my mouth open,

And they told him to masturbate,

And I, to masturbate, to jerk it,

And while we were acting like whores,

The woman soldier took her pictures.

Then they brought my friends in here,

Seven of us altogether,

And made a naked pyramid,

Piling up our bodies naked.

They took pictures also of this,

And then some more beating gave us.

After the beating they took us all

Each one to his separate cell,

And completely flooded the floor,

And told us, Lay face down in the water,

In the water, naked, without clothes,

All night like that. Face down, they left us.

In the morning, day shift issued

More clothes to wear. But, sixteen hundred,

They took the clothes away again,

When the night shift guards had come in,

And they handcuffed us to the bed,

And we had to sleep there naked.

Four night guards, two male, two female.

One of the men was wearing glasses,

Had a chain tattoo on one of his arms,

The other man had a tattoo on the skin

Of his back, it looked like a dragon.

One female also had glasses on her,

She was short and she had short hair;

The second female hair was yellow,
And she was medium height, also.

When the guards were treating me so,
I really did not know what to do;
I was trying to kill myself, but
I didn't have any way of doing it.
The guards made us crawl hands and knees
They forced us to do what they please.
They sat on our backs and rode us
As if they were riding on animals,
Others of them were taking pictures,
And writing words on our asses,
We did not understand the meaning.
They did this to us in the beginning,
The second day put us in the water,
And handcuffed us several times after.

KASIM

In God's name, now I swear to God
That every thing that I have witnessed,
Everything I here say to you,
I do not say these things for pay,
Or gain in any material thing;
I have received no pressuring,
Of any forces over me:
I choose to say what I will say.
I am only going to tell
About the Abu Ghraib Jail;
I will not talk about the others;
They were very bad, but not worse,
Than what we met at the hard site,
But you have not asked about that.

First, they stripped all my clothes off me,
Even my underwear they took away.
They gave me woman's undergarment,
That was rose color with flowers on it;
They put the bag over my face,

One of the guards he came in close,
And this one whispered in my ear,
Today I will fuck you, prisoner,
And he said this in Arabic,
That I would experience his prick,
And this was spoken to all of them,
In the first hours after we came.

They had more than one translator,
Abu Hamid, and a female soldier,
One whose skin was olive colored,
And all of these remarks were said
On October third, or near then,
Two thousand three, in the afternoon.

They took me for interrogation:
In a special cell they sat me down,
And Abu Hamid came in there
With an American soldier.
They told me I was a faggot
Because of the underwear I got,
And my answer was, No, to that.

They kept on asking me, Why then?
Why do you have this underwear on?
And I said, Because you make me,
But they never took it away.
Even when I transferred from camp B
Into the Isolation one day,
And they beat us with plastic rods,
With the black bags over our heads,
So I couldn't see their face,
And they brought us back to this place.
They forced me to have this underwear;
All the time, fifty days more,
And I tell you, most of these days,
I was not wearing anything else.

I faced more hard punishment
From the chief guard during the night.
He cuffed my hands behind my back
To the metal, the window lock,
So that my feet were off the floor,
And for five hours I just hung there;
Because I asked him what time it was,

I thought it was time for my prayers.
They took the underwear, I was naked,
And they put it over my head.
After he released me from the window,
He tied me to my bed, like so,
And left me there all the night through.
I remember the shower room.
They kept the inmates' food from them,
Although I was fasting at that time.
They took pictures of everything,
Their cameras were always flashing;
I don't know what pictures of me,
They beat me so bad I couldn't see,
I lost consciousness after an hour,
So there are things I don't remember.

They brought in three naked prisoners
Tied to each other with restraints.
They all faced towards one another,
Lying there on the concrete floor.
The soldiers were hitting them all
Over their bodies with a football.

And also the women soldiers

Stood by there taking their pictures.

I saw the head guard punch a prisoner

In the face, hard, over and over,

When the captive would not obey

And remove his underwear that day.

After the guard had beaten him,

I heard the man begging help would come,

Also the American soldiers

Told us to fuck like homosexuals;

There was a sergeant with black skin,

And seven or eight soldiers with him;

The first two days of Ramadan

They took pictures, the soldier women;

And the captives, they made them crawl

From one end to the other of the hall,

And it was very hard for them,

They were cuffed together arm to arm.

I saw one guard fucking a kid,

About fifteen or eighteen years old.

The kid was hurting very bad

They tried to conceal what they did
By hanging sheets across the door.
When I heard screaming over there
I climbed up there, and I looked in
And saw the guard in his uniform,
His pants down around his ankles,
Putting his dick in the kid's ass;
Then I couldn't see the kid's face,
But the woman soldier took pictures.
I always thought that guard was gay;
All that was in cell twenty-three.

I was right across from what they did,
In a cell on the other side.

They put the sheets on the doors again,
And cuffed the man in cell number one,
A detainee, an Iraqi citizen.
They tied him to the bed with cuffs
And inserted a phosphor in his ass;
The phosphoric light broke up
And he was yelling for God's help.

That prisoner was beaten a lot,

He was quite often getting hit:

Because we heard him screaming there.

They prohibit us standing near;

But in Ramadan, about midnight

I saw them do some more of that,

They put a stick into his ass,

And the woman took her pictures.

I saw many times the captives stand

On water buckets upside down,

And they were totally naked then;

They carried chairs over their heads,

Standing under the big fan blades,

Behind the partition over there,

And also standing in the shower.

Not one night in all my time there

Did I neglect to see or hear.

I saw and heard and felt this way,

As if these things happened to me.

Now I repeat my former oath,

I swear on Allah, this is truth,
Of all the things I said of this,
I tell you: Allah is my witness.

MOHANDED

I will start my testimony
From my first day in sector one A.
They have stripped me from my clothes there,
And of all things of the prisoner,
And I spent six days with nothing
In a helpless situation.
After three days they gave a blanket,
And then a mattress to go with it,
And with these things came in the night,
At two in the morning, approximate,
The head guard, in my open door
And a woman interrogator.
They cuffed my hands behind my back,
And my feet, so I could not walk.
They dragged me to the shower room,
And threatened all sorts of mayhem,
And then the female one left us.

And a man came, one without glasses,
Young and tall, with a thin mustache,

He started beating me very harsh!
They threw pepper into my face,
And they attacked me merciless.
This went on for a half an hour,
They started beating me with a chair,
Until, I think, the chair was broke,
And then they started to make me choke,
And at that time I thought I'd die,
It's a miracle I saw the next day.
Then they started to beat me the most,
They hit the left side of my chest,
Around my heart, to injure me
And cause bleeding internally.
Until they got tired and they quit,
And then they kicked me with their feet
And I suppose, then I passed out.

At a different scene in the night,
There was another guard in it,
He wears glasses, has a red face,
Points his gun all over the place.
He threatened many prisoners:

I never saw anything worse.

I saw things then no one should see:

They came in the morning with two,

They were father and son, we knew,

But in their hoods they could not see.

They were both naked, and they put

Them facing each other, began to count,

One, two, three, and then removed

The black bags from over their head.

When the son saw his father naked

He could not speak, he only cried,

He was so completely ashamed,

A feeling that cannot be named.

The first head guard, sometimes, at night,

Threw all our food into the toilet,

And said, Take it out and eat it.

And I saw also the captive

Who was held in room number five:

They put dogs on him, the dogs came,

They bit his leg and frightened him.

This prisoner was from Iran,

They beat him all through the prison.

HIADAR

When I first got to the hard site,
The soldiers had me in restraint.
There were two soldiers, prison guards.
A translator came in afterwards,
And Abu Hamed was his name;
In the hall when we first came in,
The guards walked up and down the line,
And they made us take off our clothes,
One after another, in nakedness;
And the chief night guard, he was there,
And an American woman soldier,
And they told me to stroke my penis
In front of her, and I did this.

Then they covered my head again,
And I obeyed every command.
I did whatever they asked of me
And they rewarded me this way:
They removed the bag from my head
And showed me my friend, where he kneeled

Right on the floor in front of me.
They told me then, Over here, sit
On the floor by the wall, facing it.
They brought another prisoner
And they placed him on my back there.
We were naked; they ordered me
To bend down on my arm and knee
With my hands spread out on the floor,
And so they piled up three others,
All naked in a pile that way;
And then they ordered me to lie,
And also they told the other guys
To lie down there on top of me
So we would all sleep in this way.
There were six of us lying there,
The guards laughed, and they took pictures.

They started stepping on our hands
And they wrote things on our bodies
In English, I could not understand it;
They took more pictures after that.
They made us walk like dogs with leash,

And the cameras they would still flash,

And we had to bark like a dog,

And if we didn't, they hit our leg,

They hit our face, they hit our chest;

No mercy, they hit us with their fist.

Then they took us back to our cells,

Only they took out the mattresses,

Threw water all over the floor,

And they made us all sleep there,

On our stomach with the bag on our head.

They took pictures of everything they did.

Some things we got from the morning guard,

He gave back our mattresses, blankets, food;

But the night guard took them away,

And this would happen every day.

That happened for ten days after,

And I know Abu Hamed was still there.

A NAMELESS PRISONER

(The name is blacked out) I am named,

And I report here how I was shamed.

I entered Abu Ghraib prison

Two thousand three, on July ten,

That was after they transferred me

From the Baghdad conflict area.

They put me into the tent first

And then they brought me to the Hard Site.

The first day here they brought me in

The dark room, where the beating began;

They started hitting at the head;

Stomach and legs, they continued.

They made me lift my hands in the air

And kneel before them on the floor.

I was like that for over four hours.

Then the Interrogator came in

And he looked on as I was beaten;

I stayed in this room for five days,

Naked, they had taken my clothes.

Then they took me to another cell,

On the upper floor, down the hall.

Fifteen October, they replaced

The Army with Iraqi police.

After this they began new ways

To make their punishment for us.

The first punishment was bringing me

To room number one. In here, they

Put their tight handcuffs on my wrist

And hung me with my arms all twisted,

For seven or eight hours I hung,

On my hand, this caused a rupturing,

My right hand had a severe cut,

It bled, and pus was coming from it.

They kept me there three days or more,

Twenty-four through twenty-six October.

Then and in all the following days

They put a dark bag over my eyes;

Also of course, this whole time through,

I was naked in everything I do,
And without any mattress, too.

One day in November we went
For a different punishment.
The American guard came in my room
And he brought five others with him.
They put the bag on me to blind me,
And cuffed my hands, and took me away.
And when we were in the hallway
Was when they started to beat me.
I could only see to their feet
From under the bag on my head.
A couple of the guards were women,
I knew, I heard their voices then,
And I saw two of the men before
They had the head bag fully secure.
There were glasses on one of them,
But he had put tape over his name
On the front of his uniform.

They made me sit down like a dog,

And lift myself up then, to beg;

Then they held the string from the bag,

And they made me bark like a dog;

And through this they would laugh at me.

One policeman was a tan color,

He hit my head to the wall there.

I saw this because when he did,

The black bag came off of my head.

Now crawl, one of the guards told me,

In Arabic, so I did as he says,

And while I crawled they spat on me,

I felt their spitting as it hit me,

And as I crawled they slapped and hit,

On my back, my head and my feet.

This treatment kept going on and on

Until four in the morning had come,

And all these same things would happen

In the following night times, again.

I remember also very clear,

The night one of them hit my ear.

It was before the usual beating,

Cuffing, bagging, leashing, and crawling.

There were six people gathered there,

And one was an Iraqi translator.

He has a mustache, he is tan;

This translator's name is Shaheen.

The police started beating me,

And they were hitting my kidneys,

When they hit me on my right ear,

It started bleeding from in there,

Then I passed out; the translator

Came and took me away from there;

I was out for about two minutes,

Maybe they used some smelling salts,

The guards came and washed off my ear,

And they called an Iraqi doctor.

He couldn't take me away with him,

So he fixed me and left me with them.

I remember some days before,

The head night guard put underwear,

Red woman's pant, over my head,

And then with the cuffs he has tied

My hands behind me to the window,

Until I passed out, hanging so.

Also one day in room number one

The head guard told me to lay down,

And I lay down on my stomach,

And the soldiers jumped on my back,

From the bed, on my back and legs,

And two of them were there spitting.

Then two of them held my hands and legs

While a third one did all these things.

They laid me out flat on the floor

And tied my hands up to the door,

Then they stood and pissed over me,

Laughing at my appearance this way.

They released my hands from the cuffs,

And I washed some of the piss off,

Then the head guard came in the room,

And he brought back a friend with him,

And they told me, Lie down over here,

And I obeyed them, out of fear,

I still had the bag on my head,

But I could feel what these men did,

One of them was opening my legs,

I could see from under the bag,

He was between my legs on his knees,

And I saw what his intention was,

He was going to do me, he was

Opening his pants for his penis,

But I started screaming loudly,

And the other guards were hitting me,

They put their feet on my neck and head,

So I couldn't scream about what he did.

Then they left and the man with glasses

Came back in the room with others,

They put me again in the dark room,

Started to beat me with a broom,

Then they put the loudspeaker on

And screamed at me through the microphone.

They broke the glowing finger open,

And spread the glowing stuff on me then.

They took me back to the other room,

And made me get down before them.

And one took the end of his stick,

The baton he carries, an inch thick,

And he stuck it inside my ass,

Up about two centimeters.

I was screaming. He pulled it out,

Took some water, and he washed it.

The two American girls came

They hit my dick with a ball of foam,

And when the guards tied me up tight,

One of the girls, she's blond and white,

Took my dick and was playing with it.

Many times inside this prison

I saw them do this to captive men,

Just as they did to me, and more.

And of all this, they took pictures.

The Ballad
Of
Anne Askew

The Ballad

Which Anne Askew
Made and Sang
When She Was a Prisoner in Newgate
And Before She Was Burned at the Stake

Like as the armèd knight
Appointed to the field,
With this world will I fight,
And faith shall be my shield.

Faith is that weapon strong
Which will not fail at need;
My foes therefor among
Therewith will I proceed.

As it is had in strength
And force of Christ's good way,
It will prevail at length,
Though devils all say nay.

Faith in the fathers old,
Obtained by righteousness,
Which makes me true and bold
To fear no world's distress.

I now rejoice in heart,
As hope bids me to do;
For Christ will take my part,
And ease me of my woe.

You say, Lord, those who knock,
To them you will attend;
Undo therefore the lock,
And your strong power send.

More enemies I have
Than hairs upon my head;
Let them not me deprave,
But fight, Lord, in my stead.

On you my care I cast,
For all their cruel spite,
And follow not their haste,
For you are my delight.

I am not she that list
My anchor to let fall,
For ev'ry driz'ling mist,
My ship substantial;

Not often do I write
In prose, nor yet in rhyme;
Yet will I show one sight
That I saw in my time:

I saw a royal throne
Where Justice should have sat;
But in her stead was one
Of muddy, cruel wit;

Absorbed was righteousness,
As of the raging flood,
Satan in his excess
Sucked up the guiltless blood;

Then thought I, Jesus, Lord,
When you shall judge us all,
Hardly will they record
What on these men will fall.

Yet Lord, I would desire,
For what they do to me,
Let them not taste the hire
Of their iniquity.

Civil Disobedience

A Song Cycle

Adapted from the essay by

Henry David Thoreau

Poems by

Jabez Van Cleef

"I will breathe the best way I know how."

"I will breathe the best way I know how."

1.

THIS GOVERNMENT, OUR EAGLE and our pledge,

What is it but American tradition,

Trying to transmit itself, intact,

Unimpaired, from past into posterity,

But at each instant of negotiation,

Shaving off some dust of its integrity?

It hasn't the vitality and force

Of a single living, breathing person.

2.

LEST WE FORGET, the standing army is

Only a portion of the standing state.

Just as an army is an instrument

Likely to be misused by the state,

The state itself, as it is deaf and blind,

Or chooses not to hear or do our will,

Is just as liable to abuse itself,

Perverting what the people might intend.

3.

I THINK THAT WE should be our best selves first,

And find our time for being subjects after.

I am not striving to obey the law;

I strive much more to emulate the right.

Law never made a soul a whit more just;

And, by means of all their due respect,

Even the well-disposed are daily made,

By what they do, the agents of injustice.

4.

THE MASS OF PEOPLE SERVE the state in silence,

Not as *souls,* but mainly as machines,

Transmitting force without excessive friction,

While their bodies grind between the gears.

They are the standing army, the militia,

Jailers and constables, *posse comitatus.*

It's likely they make no free exercise

Of their judgment or their moral sense.

5.

A VERY FEW, as heroes, patriots, martyrs,

Reformers in the greater sense, and *human*,

Serve the state with what their conscience does,

And for the most part they resist its action.

The wise one will be useful as a person,

And not submit to be dug out like clay,

Lumped and poked wherever it is needful,

To stop a hole and keep the wind away.

6.

WHEN WHOLE COUNTRIES are unjustly taken,

Conquered by an unrestrained armed force,

And people ruled by military laws,

I think that it is not a whit too soon

For honest souls to rise and revolutionize.

What makes this duty all the more compelling

Is knowing that the countries so subjected

Are not our countries. We are the invaders.

7.

IF I UNJUSTLY snatch away a plank

From the hands of someone who is drowning,

I must restore it though I drown myself;

And I say, they that would so save their lives,

In all such cases, they shall surely lose them.

I say this people must cease holding slaves,

I say we must cease making war on innocents,

Though doing this may cost us our existence.

8.

IF IMPROVEMENT of the state is slow,

It is because the few are not found wiser

Or otherwise materially better

Than the many who make up the mass.

It is not so important that the many

Should be as good as you; as that there be

Some absolute expression of the good

Somewhere; for that will leaven the whole lump.

9.

IT *IS* YOUR DUTY, at the very least,

To wash your hands of wrong where you may find it,

And, if you give it never any thought,

Not to give it, practically, your support.

If I devote myself to other things,

Pursuits and contemplations as may be,

I must first see, at least, that I do not

Sit, while pursuing, on another's shoulders.

10.

THE BROADEST & MOST PREVALENT error needs

The most disinterested virtue to sustain it.

The slight reproach sometimes elicited

By virtue of an open patriotism,

Most likely is brought down upon the virtuous.

They are the ones, who while they disapprove

The character and measures of a government,

Will yield to it allegiance and support.

11.

ACTION FROM PRINCIPLE changes what you are.

Perception and performance of the right

Is in essence revolutionary,

It is not made of things entirely new

Nor is it wholly anything which was.

Action from principle divides the state, the church,

The family, ay, divides the *individual,*

By separating devil from divine.

12.

SHALL WE BE CONTENT with our obedience?

Shall we endeavor to amend the laws

And obey them till we have succeeded?

Or, shall we transgress these laws at once?

Under such a government as this,

People mostly think they ought to wait

Until they have persuaded the majority

To alter unjust laws so they are just.

13.

WHY DOES GOVERNMENT not prize and cherish

Its wise minority, source of such improvement?

Why does it not encourage every citizen

To be on the alert, detecting faults,

And strive to *do more* than the law would have them?

Why does the government always crucify Christ,

Exile Luther and Copernicus,

Mark as rebels Washington and Franklin?

14.

I KNOW THIS WELL, that if there were one thousand,

One hundred, or ten people I could name—

If only there were ten *honest* souls—

If ONE HONEST PERSON, in this our State

Of Massachusetts, *ceasing to hold slaves,*

Would actually withdraw from this copartnership,

And be locked in the county jail therefor,

It would abolish slavery in America.

15.

IT IS IN PRISON that the fugitive slave,

And the Mexican prisoner on parole,

And the Indian, come to plead all wrongs,

Should find themselves within the pale of right;

A separate, free and honorable ground,

Where the State puts those who are not *with* her,

It is the only house in a slave State

In which a free man can abide with honor.

16.

IF ANY THINK THEIR INFLUENCE would be lost,

By being generally thought an enemy

Within the walls of that state where they dwell,

They do not know by how much more is truth

Stronger than the error of injustice,

Nor how much more with truth and eloquence

A prisoner can combat and break injustice

Who has received the news of it in person.

17.

LET PEACEFUL REVOLUTION be accomplished:

But even if domestic blood should flow,

Is there not a sort of blood that's shed

When the conscience of a soul is wounded?

Out of this wound I think that real humanity,

A soul's real immortality, escapes;

We bleed there to an everlasting death.

I see this blood is flowing from us now.

18.

I SAW THAT, IF THERE WERE A WALL of stone

There between me and my fellow townsfolk,

There was a still more daunting rock to climb

Or to break through, or perhaps to tunnel,

Before they could know freedom as I did.

I did not in prison feel confined,

And the walls and bars they put around me

Seemed a great waste of stone and iron and mortar.

19.

AS THEY COULD NOT REACH ME in my spirit,

They had resolved to punish just my body;

As boys, if they cannot come at some person

Whom they wish to spite, abuse a dog.

I saw the State in person as half-witted,

Timid as a crone with silver spoons,

It did not know its allies from its foes,

And I lost all respect for it, and pitied it.

20.

AND EVER THUS THE STATE AVOIDS confronting

Our senses, intellectual or moral,

But only with intent assaults the body.

It offers not superior wit or honesty,

But it applies superior physical strength.

I was not born to answer physical force.

I will breathe the best way I know how.

Let us between us see who is the stronger.

21.

I PERCEIVE TWO nuts fall side by side,

Suppose they are an acorn and a chestnut;

One does not give leave or serve the other,

But both obey their own laws, spring and grow,

And both will try to flourish as they may,

Till one, perchance, may shadow o'er the other.

If a plant cannot thrive by its nature,

Then it dies; and so with people too.

∞

Chidiok Tichborne's Lament

Chidiok Tichborne, a member of Babington's
Conspiracy, wrote this poem in the Tower of London on
the night before his execution:

My prime of youth is but a frost of cares,

My feast of joy is but a dish of pain,

My crop of corn is but a field of tares,

And all my good is but vain hope of gain.

The day is gone and I yet I saw no sun,

And now I live, and now my life is done.

The spring is past, and yet it hath not sprung,

The fruit is dead, and yet the leaves are green,

My youth is gone, and yet I am but young,

I saw the world, and yet I was not seen,

My thread is cut, and yet it was not spun,

And now I live, and now my life is done.

I sought my death and found it in my womb,

I look't for life and saw it was a shade,

I trod the earth and knew it was my tomb,

And now I die, and now I am but made.

The glass is full, and now the glass is run,

And now I live, and now my life is done.

This wall of stone is nothing more than air

And all of time and space before me lie

For if, in future age, some souls there be,

Who little know my circumstance or care,

Yet read these words, and hear my music true,

Then I can rest, for I will still be there.

The Universal Declaration
Of Human Rights

The Universal Declaration of Human Rights

On December 10, 1948 the General Assembly of the
United Nations adopted and proclaimed the Universal
Declaration of Human Rights the full text of which
appears in the following pages. Following this historic act
the Assembly called upon all Member countries to
publicize the text of the Declaration and "to cause it to be
disseminated, displayed, read and expounded principally
in schools and other educational institutions, without
distinction based on the political status of countries or
territories."

PREAMBLE

Whereas recognition of the inherent dignity and
of the equal and inalienable rights of all members
of the human family is the foundation of freedom,
justice and peace in the world,

Whereas disregard and contempt for human
rights have resulted in barbarous acts which have
outraged the conscience of mankind, and the
advent of a world in which human beings shall
enjoy freedom of speech and belief and freedom
from fear and want has been proclaimed as the
highest aspiration of the common people,

Whereas it is essential, if man is not to be
compelled to have recourse, as a last resort, to
rebellion against tyranny and oppression, that

human rights should be protected by the rule of law,

Whereas it is essential to promote the development of friendly relations between nations,

Whereas the peoples of the United Nations have in the Charter reaffirmed their faith in fundamental human rights, in the dignity and worth of the human person and in the equal rights of men and women and have determined to promote social progress and better standards of life in larger freedom,

Whereas Member States have pledged themselves to achieve, in co-operation with the United Nations, the promotion of universal respect for and observance of human rights and fundamental freedoms,

Whereas a common understanding of these rights and freedoms is of the greatest importance for the full realization of this pledge,

Now, Therefore THE GENERAL ASSEMBLY proclaims THIS UNIVERSAL DECLARATION OF HUMAN RIGHTS as a common standard of achievement for all peoples and all nations, to the end that every individual and every organ of society, keeping this Declaration constantly in mind, shall strive by teaching and education to promote respect for these rights and freedoms and by progressive measures, national and international, to secure their universal and effective recognition and observance, both among the peoples of Member States themselves and among the peoples of territories under their jurisdiction.

Article 1.

All human beings are born free and equal in dignity and rights. They are endowed with reason and conscience and should act towards one another in a spirit of brotherhood.

Article 2.

Everyone is entitled to all the rights and freedoms set forth in this Declaration, without distinction of any kind, such as race, colour, sex, language, religion, political or other opinion, national or social origin, property, birth or other status. Furthermore, no distinction shall be made on the basis of the political, jurisdictional or international status of the country or territory to which a person belongs, whether it be independent, trust, non-self-governing or under any other limitation of sovereignty.

Article 3.

Everyone has the right to life, liberty and security of person.

Article 4.

No one shall be held in slavery or servitude; slavery and the slave trade shall be prohibited in all their forms.

Article 5.

No one shall be subjected to torture or to cruel, inhuman or degrading treatment or punishment.

Article 6.

Everyone has the right to recognition everywhere as a person before the law.

Article 7.

All are equal before the law and are entitled without any discrimination to equal protection of the law. All are entitled to equal protection against any discrimination in violation of this Declaration and against any incitement to such discrimination.

Article 8.

Everyone has the right to an effective remedy by the competent national tribunals for acts violating the fundamental rights granted him by the constitution or by law.

Article 9.

No one shall be subjected to arbitrary arrest, detention or exile.

Article 10.

Everyone is entitled in full equality to a fair and public hearing by an independent and impartial tribunal, in the determination of his rights and obligations and of any criminal charge against him.

Article 11.

(1) Everyone charged with a penal offence has the right to be presumed innocent until proved guilty according to law in a public trial at which he has had all the guarantees necessary for his defense.
(2) No one shall be held guilty of any penal offence on account of any act or omission which

did not constitute a penal offence, under national or international law, at the time when it was committed. Nor shall a heavier penalty be imposed than the one that was applicable at the time the penal offence was committed.

Article 12.

No one shall be subjected to arbitrary interference with his privacy, family, home or correspondence, nor to attacks upon his honor and reputation. Everyone has the right to the protection of the law against such interference or attacks.

Article 13.

(1) Everyone has the right to freedom of movement and residence within the borders of each state.

(2) Everyone has the right to leave any country, including his own, and to return to his country.

Article 14.

(1) Everyone has the right to seek and to enjoy in other countries asylum from persecution.

(2) This right may not be invoked in the case of prosecutions genuinely arising from non-political crimes or from acts contrary to the purposes and principles of the United Nations.

Article 15.

(1) Everyone has the right to a nationality.

(2) No one shall be arbitrarily deprived of his nationality nor denied the right to change his nationality.

Article 16.

(1) Men and women of full age, without any limitation due to race, nationality or religion, have

the right to marry and to found a family. They are entitled to equal rights as to marriage, during marriage and at its dissolution.

(2) Marriage shall be entered into only with the free and full consent of the intending spouses.

(3) The family is the natural and fundamental group unit of society and is entitled to protection by society and the State.

Article 17.

(1) Everyone has the right to own property alone as well as in association with others.

(2) No one shall be arbitrarily deprived of his property.

Article 18.

Everyone has the right to freedom of thought, conscience and religion; this right includes freedom to change his religion or belief, and freedom, either alone or in community with others and in public or private, to manifest his religion or belief in teaching, practice, worship and observance.

Article 19.

Everyone has the right to freedom of opinion and expression; this right includes freedom to hold opinions without interference and to seek, receive and impart information and ideas through any media and regardless of frontiers.

Article 20.

(1) Everyone has the right to freedom of peaceful assembly and association.

(2) No one may be compelled to belong to an association.

Article 21.

(1) Everyone has the right to take part in the government of his country, directly or through freely chosen representatives.

(2) Everyone has the right of equal access to public service in his country.

(3) The will of the people shall be the basis of the authority of government; this will shall be expressed in periodic and genuine elections which shall be by universal and equal suffrage and shall be held by secret vote or by equivalent free voting procedures.

Article 22.

Everyone, as a member of society, has the right to social security and is entitled to realization, through national effort and international co-operation and in accordance with the organization and resources of each State, of the economic, social and cultural rights indispensable for his dignity and the free development of his personality.

Article 23.

(1) Everyone has the right to work, to free choice of employment, to just and favorable conditions of work and to protection against unemployment.

(2) Everyone, without any discrimination, has the right to equal pay for equal work.

(3) Everyone who works has the right to just and favorable remuneration ensuring for himself and his family an existence worthy of human dignity, and supplemented, if necessary, by other means of social protection.

(4) Everyone has the right to form and to join trade unions for the protection of his interests.

Article 24.

Everyone has the right to rest and leisure, including reasonable limitation of working hours and periodic holidays with pay.

Article 25.

(1) Everyone has the right to a standard of living adequate for the health and well-being of himself and of his family, including food, clothing, housing and medical care and necessary social services, and the right to security in the event of unemployment, sickness, disability, widowhood, old age or other lack of livelihood in circumstances beyond his control.

(2) Motherhood and childhood are entitled to special care and assistance. All children, whether born in or out of wedlock, shall enjoy the same social protection.

Article 26.

(1) Everyone has the right to education. Education shall be free, at least in the elementary and fundamental stages. Elementary education shall be compulsory. Technical and professional education shall be made generally available and higher education shall be equally accessible to all on the basis of merit.

(2) Education shall be directed to the full development of the human personality and to the strengthening of respect for human rights and fundamental freedoms. It shall promote understanding, tolerance and friendship among all

nations, racial or religious groups, and shall further the activities of the United Nations for the maintenance of peace.

(3) Parents have a prior right to choose the kind of education that shall be given to their children.

Article 27.

(1) Everyone has the right freely to participate in the cultural life of the community, to enjoy the arts and to share in scientific advancement and its benefits.

(2) Everyone has the right to the protection of the moral and material interests resulting from any scientific, literary or artistic production of which he is the author.

Article 28.

Everyone is entitled to a social and international order in which the rights and freedoms set forth in this Declaration can be fully realized.

Article 29.

(1) Everyone has duties to the community in which alone the free and full development of his personality is possible.

(2) In the exercise of his rights and freedoms, everyone shall be subject only to such limitations as are determined by law solely for the purpose of securing due recognition and respect for the rights and freedoms of others and of meeting the just requirements of morality, public order and the general welfare in a democratic society.

(3) These rights and freedoms may in no case be exercised contrary to the purposes and principles of the United Nations.

Article 30.

Nothing in this Declaration may be interpreted as implying for any State, group or person any right to engage in any activity or to perform any act aimed at the destruction of any of the rights and freedoms set forth herein.

A Note on Singing Texts

The texts in this book may be set to tunes and sung. On the following pages I have made sample arrangements of two poems taken from "Songs of Civil Disobedience." The music is four-part Anglican chant (tunes are in the public domain). Points have been inserted in the text to help singers align the words with the notes.

1.

THIS GOVERNMENT, OUR EAGLE · and our ·
pledge,
What is it but A · meri · can trad · ition,

Trying to transmit it · self, in · tact,
Unimpaired, from · past in · to pos · terity,

But at each instant of ne · goti · ation,
Shaving off some · dust of · its in · tegrity?

It hasn't the vi · tality and · force
Of a single · living, · breathing · person.

17.

LET PEACEFUL REVOLUTION · be ac ·
complished:
Even if our · people's · blood should · flow,

Is there not a sort of · blood that's · shed,
When the conscience · of a · soul is ·
wounded?

Out of this wound I think that · real hu · manity,
A soul's real immor · tali · ty, e · scapes;

We bleed there to an ever · lasting · death.
I see this blood is · flowing · from us · now.